AUDUBON

Painter of Birds in the Wild Frontier

by JENNIFER ARMSTRONG

illustrations by JOS. A. SMITH

Harry N. Abrams, Inc., Publishers

John James Audubon and his horse, Barro, dawdled up the trail through the trees. January 1812 was cold and gray in the Kentucky wilderness, and there was not another soul on the path. Ahead, the sky was darkening, and there was a distant grumble, like thunder.

Birds of all colors and sizes flitted in and out of winter shadows. Audubon knew all their names. He knew all their songs. He knew their eggs and their nests. He knew what they ate and what ate them.

An orange oriole flashed across the trail and lit on a swaying blackberry cane. A mockingbird sang in a hickory tree. The frontier was chock-full of birds, but as the afternoon sky darkened, the birds grew strangely still.

Audubon's horse, Barro, began to slow down. He placed one foot down, then another, and then dropped his head and groaned.

Audubon was alarmed. Could Barro be sick? Just as he made ready to dismount, he saw the trees around him tremble.

Barro groaned again and braced himself. Audubon stared. The ground was moving, rippling like water! Birds burst from the undergrowth, their cries lost in the thrashing of branches. Audubon clutched the reins as the world rattled and rumbled.

And then the earthquake was over.

His heart racing, Audubon patted the folder strapped to Barro's back.

Safe. It was safe. It was a large, leather folder, tied with ribbon. Inside were paintings and drawings. There were pictures of swans. Sketches of warblers. Paintings of kingfishers and robins and bluebirds and Carolina parakeets. There were birds the scientists had not even given names to yet. America was young, and the western wilderness was filled with animals and plants unknown back East.

Audubon knew more birds than anyone else on the frontier. He studied them. He hunted them so that he could examine every detail of feather and claw. And when he knew every last thing about each bird, he painted it.

His paintings were unusual, so lifelike and accurate that a viewer might expect the birds to squawk and preen their feathers. Audubon had the beginnings of an idea just testing its wings in his imagination: if he could paint all the birds of America in life size, he would have done something remarkable.

Painting all the birds of America was hard work, however. His dream had taken him into swamps and blizzards. It had sent him up rivers. He had climbed mountains, faced down bears, made friends with the Shawnee and the Osage tribes, and now he had withstood an earthquake in the wilderness. But of course, nobody changed the world without a little effort.

When this dreamer and painter of birds had started life, who could have imagined him riding up this lonesome frosty trail? John James Audubon was born the son of a wealthy French planter in the West Indies. He spent much of his youth in France, and then in French Louisiana. He could paint, dance, and play the flute and the violin—just the right sort of pastimes for a gentleman.

But he was also a crack shot with a rifle. He loved to explore the woods and study the habits of birds and make pictures of them.

By the time he was a young man, he was in charge of a Pennsylvania farm that belonged to his father. Very little of his attention was spent on the farm, however. He just was not a farmer by nature. Audubon's wandering feet took him into the countryside and the woodlands at every chance.

He was made for adventure, and America in 1804 was the place to find it. The United States had just bought an enormous piece of land out past the Mississippi River. Men and women everywhere were dreaming of this wild American frontier.

Luckily for Audubon, his sweetheart dreamed of the frontier, too. So Audubon and a partner named Ferdinand Rozier agreed to go into business. They would move to Kentucky and open a general store. Audubon could send for his daring bride, Lucy, when he was settled.

Getting to Kentucky was the first adventure. It took days in a stagecoach and then a long journey down the twisting Ohio River in a keelboat. The wilderness stretched into the distance on both sides of the river. Audubon sat on the deck of the boat with a sketchbook and drew everything he saw.

It was Paradise! So much wildlife! So many birds, so many trees and flowers! Everything grew in huge numbers and great sizes.

But nothing could compare to the flocks of passenger pigeons. One afternoon, as Audubon sat sketching, the sky grew dark. A strange roar came faintly on the wind. The boatmen stopped trading tall tales for a moment and paused to listen.

Then, like a tornado or a mighty thundercloud, the pigeons came. The sky was black with them, as far as the eye could see. Their calls deafened the ear. Audubon tried to guess how many birds there were. Ten thousand? One hundred thousand? A million?

They came in huge flocks, one after the other. Audubon began to count. Each time a flock passed overhead, he marked his sketchbook with a dot. For twenty-one minutes he gazed upward, checking off the flocks as they passed.

When he stopped to count how many he had seen, the total was 160—
and they were still passing overhead!

How many birds were in *each* of those flocks? Audubon shook his head
in wonderment. The deck of the boat was covered in bird droppings, and
he skidded as he walked. He hardly noticed, however. He was too amazed.
The flocks continued passing overhead for hours and hours.

This was the American wilderness, Audubon marveled. Stupendous,
miraculous, awesome!

Louisville, Kentucky, was already an important town on the Ohio River in 1808 when Audubon and his partner opened a new store. One business enterprise in Kentucky had already failed, but America was a place for one new start after another.

Restless Audubon however never could stand still to sell flour or nails, hams or hardware. When he should have been tending business, Audubon roamed in the woods. Instead of minding the store, he hunted or fished, or watched and drew birds.

One evening, as the sun sank behind the oaks and butternuts, Audubon noticed thousands of swifts flying overhead. One by one, they flew straight as arrows toward a giant sycamore. One by one, they dove into a hole in its side.

Audubon ran to the tree and pressed his ear to the trunk. From inside came a great whirring and roaring. What he heard was the noise made by an enormous crowd of birds roosting inside the hollow tree. Why, this sycamore was *packed* with swifts!

Too excited to go home, the painter stayed the night in the woods. When the sun rose, the birds poured out of the tree like smoke. Audubon stood dumbstruck.

He had to see the inside of this gigantic bird colony. Audubon hurried home, and when he returned with a saw, he carefully cut a trapdoor in the base of the tree and crawled through.

Once inside, he crouched in a thick pile of dry bird droppings and raised his lantern. Through a cloud of drifting feathers, he saw that every square inch of the trunk was lined with nests. As he waited for the swifts to return, he counted nests and made a few calculations in his head. By his reckoning, 9,000 birds roosted in that one huge sycamore every night.

And when all 9,000 swifts returned that evening, Audubon was among them. He stood in a tornado of graceful, twittering birds, his heart soaring.

Audubon recorded that one cool night in 1810, an old gent in buck-skins arrived at a house in the Kentucky woods where the artist was visiting. Leaning his rifle against the fireplace, the man took off his coonskin hat and slapped the dust from it. Audubon set down his violin and welcomed the stranger. That was frontier hospitality.

The newcomer put out his hand and introduced himself as Boone.

Audubon's eyes widened in the lamplight. This old, careworn man was the great frontiersman, Daniel Boone!

The two began talking about life in the woods. They talked about hunting and tracking. They talked about weather and politics. They talked about Audubon's bird paintings. Audubon said he wished he knew how to shoot birds without spoiling their feathers.

Boone nodded. He would teach Audubon how to "bark" squirrels, he promised. It might be a good way to collect birds to study.

The next day, Boone and Audubon took their rifles into the woods. Dry leaves crunched under their moccasins. Blue jays scolded from the butternut trees.

Boone pointed to a squirrel sitting in the crook of a tree. Slowly he raised his long rifle. He took careful aim and shot the trunk just below the animal. Bark flew into pieces, and the squirrel dropped dead from shock, without a nick or a scratch on it.

That was barking, Boone said. Audubon bowed and thanked his new friend. He was mighty pleased to know how to take birds without damaging the plumage.

Boone stuck around for a few days and then said he had to get on home to Missouri. He put his rifle over his shoulder and headed up the trail. The old man in buckskins blended into the underbrush like a quail or a whippoorwill. One moment he was there, and the next he was gone.

In the fall not long after, Audubon and his partner, Rozier, headed up the Mississippi River to Sainte Genevieve. They had extra supplies to sell, and they thought this small river town would welcome a couple of merchants.

(In fact, Audubon went on the trip for another reason he did not tell his partner. He hoped to see trumpeter swans and eagles along the way. He did not yet have any good pictures of them, and he felt the lack in his collection.)

Winter was coming down quick, however. The keelboat captain was
none too pleased with the look of the sky. Lazy snowflakes floated to the
ground like feathers from a fat white goose. Chunks of ice bobbed like
ducks down the gray waters of the Mississippi.

Sure enough, winter caught the keelboat on the river. Audubon,
Rozier, and the whole crew set up a camp on the shore and prepared
to wait for a thaw. But that might be weeks.

Rozier grumbled about the long delay and bundled himself into a buffalo robe. But Audubon was elated. What did he care if business was put off? He did not care about the business at all anyway! He whistled as he helped set up the camp.

Nearby was a camp of Shawnee. Audubon always welcomed the chance to talk to the native people and to learn what they knew about the birds and other wildlife. He felt sure to see the swans he wanted, now that he had the time to search for them.

The river was frozen where the camp was, and Audubon could walk easily from shore to shore. He prowled the countryside on both banks with his rifle and his sketchbook, hunting game and drawing birds.

One afternoon as he came back to the river, he saw the ice covered with immense flocks of trumpeter swans, and he ducked behind a bare tree to observe them, his prize in sight. At last, the very birds he was looking for! But what were they doing? Not one of them made a sound. The magnificent white birds all lay flat on the ice, their necks stretched out, staring in the same direction. Audubon watched them watch the far shore.

There, slipping in and out of the shadows, were wolves.

Ten wolves. Twenty wolves. Audubon lost count as they moved forward onto the ice.

Still, the snowy white birds made not a sound. They did not move a feather. Were they frozen with cold or fear?

The wolves crept forward, heads low, eyes on the fat swans. Audubon held his breath.

And then, in a cloud of thundering wings, the swans burst from the ice in unison. They pounded the air above the wolves, trumpeting loudly.

The terrified wolves turned tail and dashed back into the safety of the woods, their dinner gone. Audubon laughed and laughed. His laughter followed the immense white cloud of swans as they disappeared in the winter sky.

He could not wait to paint what he had seen!

Author's Note

I chose to write about John James Audubon (1785–1851) because of my interest in America's pioneer naturalists, who braved uncharted swamps, forests, mountains, and plains in search of animals and plants not yet known to science.

Audubon explored the wilderness for many, many years, but the adventures recounted in this book all took place between 1804 and 1812. However, the day that Audubon counted the passenger pigeons was actually several months after the earthquake. I made that small change to create more drama. By the way, the earthquake that upset his horse so badly was one of the largest recorded to shake North America. Its center was New Madrid, Missouri, and it was strong enough to make the mighty Mississippi River run *backward*.

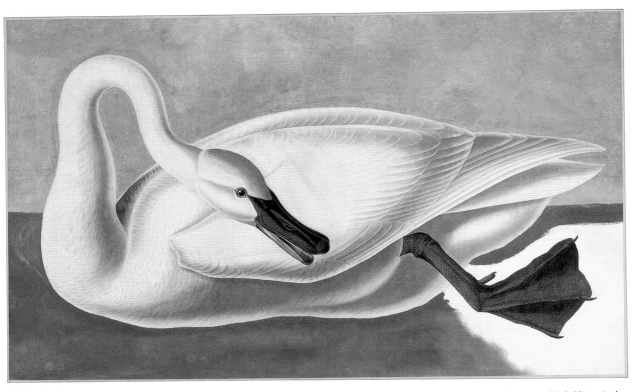

Trumpeter Swan, ca. 1836-1837. Watercolor, pastel, oil paint, and graphite on paper, 38 x 52 in. Collection of The New-York Historical Society, 1863.17.406.

The details of Audubon's life told here are taken from his personal diaries. Among the books I read to supplement his journals were Shirley Streshinsky's biography for adults, *Audubon: Life and Art in the American Wilderness*. For young readers I would also recommend these books: *John James Audubon* by Joseph Kastner, *John James Audubon: Artist of the Wild* by Martha E. Kendall, and *John James Audubon, Wildlife Artist* by Peter Anderson. Over the years, art historians have questioned and, in fact, have discredited some of the stories that Audubon claimed were true. As we do with the exploits of other great American adventurers, we must speculate that probably part is true and part myth. However, Audubon's important contribution to art and to natural history go unchallenged.

Audubon's extraordinary artistic talent and his skill and dedication in observing wildlife have made him one of history's greatest painters of birds and animals. His quest for accurately reproducing the shades and hues of feathers led him to experiment with techniques, using pencil, ink, pastel chalk, oil paint, and watercolors—sometimes using a mixture of these within a single painting. It

The paintings illustrating the Author and Artist Notes are reproductions of Audubon's originals. The artist was a ruthless critic of himself and often destroyed paintings that dissatisfied him; or he would redo them; or even cut up and paste together pieces of his works to make a new painting.

Northern Oriole, 1822-1825. Watercolor, gouache, pastel, and graphite on paper, 27 x 35 in. Collection of The New-York Historical Society, 1863.17.12.

was a meeting with the famed naturalist and bird-watcher, Alexander Wilson, in 1810 that gave Audubon the idea of publishing his bird portraits. In 1820 he decided once and for all to quit business and make painting his lifetime's work. In 1826 Audubon traveled to England with some of his drawings in order to find a publisher who could do justice to his pictures. His monumental *The Birds of America* was published in four volumes between 1827 and 1838 and contained 1065 birds. Because the birds were rendered life-sized, the book had to be published on the largest paper available, called an elephant folio, 39½ inches by 29½ inches. For example, Audubon depicted the trumpeter swan (facing page), as well as other large and long-necked birds (flamingos, herons, etc.) as a single specimen occupying the whole page; its bent posture, with its long neck turned down, allows it to fit within the dimensions of the paper. By contrast, the painting of the Orioles (above), much smaller birds, shows them perched on a tulip tree. The book was huge and expensive, with the paintings reproduced by engraving and colored in by hand. Critics were astonished. The great French naturalist Georges Cuvier proclaimed Audubon's paintings the finest of their kind anywhere.

Audubon became the most famous bird painter the world has ever seen, as well as one of the most famous naturalists. The Audubon Society, formed for the study and preservation of birds, is named in his honor. Yes, Audubon did shoot the birds he painted, but only out of his zeal for scientific and artistic study. The Audubon Society now protects the birds he hunted. Two of the birds mentioned in this book are now extinct: the Carolina parakeet, which used to dress up the woods of the American South, and the passenger pigeon, which used to blacken the sky by the millions.

ARTIST'S NOTE

Some books are more of a challenge to illustrate than others. This book is definitely one of the difficult ones. Many of the scenes in the book describe things that none of us will ever see. What must it have been like to see flocks of passenger pigeons so numerous they blocked the sun and turned the day to night? What would it be like to crawl inside of a huge, hollow tree and be surrounded by thousands of swirling swifts?

There are no photographs of Audubon or the things that he saw. I did not use models or many direct references in creating these paintings, rather I imagined what the scene must have been and painted from these imaginings. However, I did have solid picture reference for a number of objects such as the keelboats, rifles, and contemporary dress. For Audubon himself I had access to his self-portait from his sketchbook, depicting him in buckskins and a coonskin hat with a visor. Also I used portraits painted by his sons (which also gave me reference for the artist's horse). For the Shawnee people that Audubon met, I found accurate clothing and models on the Shawnee Reservation website. And of course for the many birds, I used my facsimile copy of *Birds of America* and *Birding* magazine.

Left: *Passenger Pigeon*, ca. 1824.
Watercolor, gouache, and graphite, 26 x 18 in.
Collection of The New-York Historical Society,
1863.17.062.

Above: *Chimney Swift*, ca. 1824; 1829. Watercolor,
gouache, collage, and graphite on paper, 28 x 22 in.
Collection of The New-York Historical Society,
1863.17.158.

This portrait of Audubon, made when the artist was in his mid-fifties, was painted by his son, John Woodhouse.

J. Woodhouse Audubon. *John James Audubon*, ca. 1840-41. Oil on linen, 44 x 35 in. Collection of The New-York Historical Society, 1974.46.

Reading about Audubon I discovered many interesting facts: he not only could paint with both hands but at the same time! This allowed him to work quickly. Needless to say, I did not try to imitate that particular feat, although I did depict him working with a brush in each hand. He admitted in 1827, "No one, I think, paints in my method; I, who have never studied but by piece-meal, form my pictures according to my ways of study." His work improved quickly over time, however, and is a staggering accomplishment—artistically and scientifically.

Audubon was a consummate PR man and invented fantastic stories about himself to boost sales. He claimed to be a son of King Louis XVI of France, that he was a student of Jacques-Louis David, and that he hunted with Daniel Boone. Whether he ever did meet Boone is still questioned.

I did the illustrations in watercolor on paper with occasional touches of pencil, watercolor pencil, and pen and ink. The watercolors were done exactly the same size as you see them in the book. Although pen is easier to control, I prefer the struggle to control the tip of the paint brush to create detail. Unlike computer-generated images that rely on scanned photographs, I like the feel of "home-made" images using paint and pencil. This book combines history and imagination and was an adventure.

In memory of the first naturalist in my life, Mr. G.

—J.A.

For my father, George L. Smith, who sat by my bed night after night when I was a child with

mumps, reading me the biography of John James Audubon—and made me want to be an artist.

—J.A.S.

Designer: Edward Miller
Production Manager: Hope Koturo

Library of Congress Cataloging-in-Publication Data

Armstrong, Jennifer.
  Audubon : painter of birds in the wild frontier / by Jennifer
Armstrong ; illustrated by Jos. A. Smith.
      p. cm.
Summary: Briefly tells the story of this nineteenth-century painter and
naturalist who is most famous for his detailed paintings of birds.
  ISBN 0-8109-4238-0
  1. Audubon, John James, 1785-1851—Juvenile literature. 2.
Ornithologists—United States—Biography—Juvenile literature. 3.
Animal painters—United States—Biography—Juvenile literature. [1.
Audubon, John James, 1785-1851. 2. Naturalists. 3. Artists.] I. Smith,
Joseph A. (Joseph Anthony), 1936- ill. II. Title.

QL31.A9 A69 2003
598'.092—dc21
                                    2002011921

Printed in Singapore
10 9 8 7 6 5 4 3 2 1

Harry N. Abrams, Inc.
100 Fifth Avenue
New York, N.Y. 10011
www.abramsbooks.com

Abrams is a subsidiary of